BUTTERFLY

By William Anthony

How Things Grow

PowerKiDS press

Published in 2023 by The Rosen Publishing Group, Inc.
2544 Clinton Street, Buffalo, NY 14224

Written by: William Anthony
Edited by: Robin Twiddy
Designed by: Jasmine Pointer & Amy Li

Photo credits: Images are courtesy of Shutterstock.com. With thanks to Getty Images, Thinkstock Photo, and iStockphoto. Additional illustrations by Jasmine Pointer.

Front cover – Alesia-Susie, Alex Romanjski, Bryan St Croix, K Hanley CHDPhoto. Recurring images – Alesia Susie, ilnazgilov, Maria Skrigan. Internals – Colorfuel Studio, MarcusVDT, Ebtikar, Candy_Plus, Tartila, Ewa-Saks, Vach cameraman, Bibadash, Cosmin Manci, Keith Hider, Park Ji Sun, hwongcc, kingfisher, torook, Bedrich Hrstka.

Cataloging-in-Publication Data

Names: Anthony, William.
Title: Butterfly / William Anthony.
Description: New York : Powerkids Press, 2023. | Series: How things grow |
Identifiers: ISBN 9781538389898 (pbk.) | ISBN 9781538389911 (library bound) |
ISBN 9781538389928 (ebook)
Subjects: LCSH: Butterflies--Juvenile literature. | Butterflies--Life cycles--Juvenile literature. |
Butterflies--Metamorphosis--Juvenile literature.
Classification: LCC QL544.2 A67 2023 | DDC 595.7'89156--dc23

Manufactured in the United States of America

CPSIA Compliance Information: Batch #CWPK23. For further information contact Rosen Publishing at 1-800-237-9932.

Can you follow the

instructions

in this book to see how a butterfly grows?

You are a living thing.

Plants and animals are living things too.

Living things **grow** as they get older.

A butterfly is a living thing.
But it starts life as something different.

Turn over

this leaf to see how a butterfly starts its life...

They are safely hidden under the leaf.

Can you

tap

one of the eggs
to help it hatch?

Wait!

That is not a butterfly!

It is a caterpillar!

Can you

count

how many colors
this caterpillar has?

This baby caterpillar is hungry.

It needs to eat leaves.

Can you

make a path

from leaf to leaf

for the caterpillar?

The caterpillar is growing!
It grows out of its old skin.

Wiggle

the book to help the caterpillar wriggle out of its old skin!

Perfect! Now, the caterpillar finds a safe spot.

Then, it turns into a pupa.

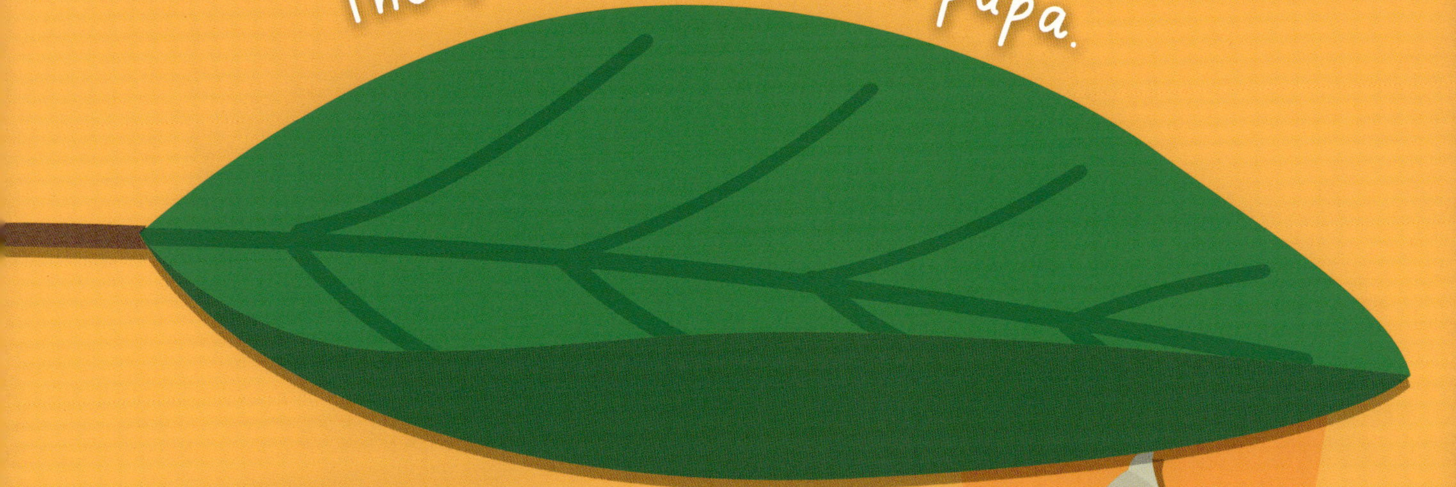

Can you

spot

the pupa on this page?

It is hidden well!

Good spot!

Inside, the caterpillar is changing.

It is changing into a butterfly.

Can you

spin

this book to make the caterpillar change?

Look! The butterfly has broken out of the case.

Look at its wings!

Can you

stretch out

your arms like a butterfly's wings?

The butterfly is ready to fly away.

Can you

open

and **close**

this page to make the butterfly's wings flap?

That is how a butterfly grows!
Can you put these stages in order?